Original title:
Paradise Found at Sea

Copyright © 2025 Creative Arts Management OÜ
All rights reserved.

Author: Giselle Montgomery
ISBN HARDBACK: 978-1-80581-605-8
ISBN PAPERBACK: 978-1-80581-132-9
ISBN EBOOK: 978-1-80581-605-8

Oasis of Serenity Amidst the Caspian

Waves like giggles bounce along,
A seal sings off-key, but strong.
With flip-flops on a warrior's feet,
We're surfing snacks, not waves, how neat!

Seagulls squabble over chips,
While sipping drinks and doing flips.
The sunset paints with silly strokes,
As mermaids laugh and share their jokes.

The Vows of Salt and Sun

Under the sun, we take our vows,
Next to a crab who slowly bows.
A halo made of seaweed sways,
As fish become our wedding bouquet.

With sand between our silly toes,
We dance a jig, and off it goes.
A starfish claps, the shells applaud,
While dolphins shout, 'Get hitched, you odd!'

Cornucopia of Currents and Colors

In boats adorned with bright confetti,
We sail through sea-spiced spaghetti.
The fishes wear their finest hats,
While jellyfish dance like silly cats.

Riding waves, we find our groove,
Yelling 'Wheee!' with every move.
A conch shell plays our funny song,
While dolphins join, and we sing along.

Daydreaming on Serene Sands

Lying back in soft, warm grains,
I dream of squids in silly chains.
The tide pulls tricks, a teasing game,
And just like that, I'm not the same.

Seagulls drop their food with flair,
While sunbathers pretend to care.
A sandcastle stands tall and proud,
Until the tide says, 'Not allowed!'

Journeys to the Liquid Horizon

On a boat made of noodles, we surfed on a wave,
A seagull stole my sandwich, oh how I behaved!
With a fish on my line, I tried to be sly,
It jumped in a tutu, said, "Catch me if you can!"

We danced with the dolphins, they laughed as they twirled,
But one tried to text me, his fins all unfurled.
He asked for a selfie, said I was the star,
I replied, "Stick to swimming, you'll go far!"

The sun wore sunglasses, so cool and so bright,
While my hat flew away in the heat of the night.
The waves told me secrets, they giggled with glee,
As I dove for a treasure, a chest full of tea!

As the tide rolled in, we built castles of foam,
With jellyfish guards, they all called it their home.
I pondered the meaning of life in a wave,
And thought, "I should've brought snacks, I'm not very brave!"

Songs of Abyssal Bliss

Underwater disco, where fish start to groove,
They're wearing tiny hats and they really can move!
An octopus DJ spinning tunes with eight hands,
Spouts bubbles of laughter, oh how he commands!

I swam with the turtles, they rapped by the reef,
Sharing tales of the ocean, all in disbelief.
A crab tried to dance, but lost both of his shoes,
He declared, "Let's do cha-cha underwater blues!"

With a wink from a whale, he sang to the crowd,
His voice made the dolphins jump up, oh so proud!
They hit the sea floor, with splashes and spins,
While I ordered a cocktail that came with fish fins!

The jellyfish glow like a strobe light at night,
While snails slide on by, moving slow, feeling right.
We toasted with clams as the stars shined above,
And laughed till we cried, oh the sea, how we love!

The Mermaid's Celestial Call

A mermaid swam with a starry pout,
She sang of fish that wouldn't spout.
With bubbles bursting in the sun,
She giggled wetly, 'Aren't we fun?'

Her scales shimmered, all glitzy and bright,
She waved at crabs that scurried in fright.
'The ocean's my stage,' she declared with glee,
'Who needs a land when you've got a sea?'

Serenade of Soft Crests

Waves rolled in with a gentle tease,
Turning seashells into great big cheese.
Seagulls squawked their own quirky tune,
While fishes danced beneath the moon.

A crab played jazz on the sandy floor,
Tapping his claws, wanting more and more.
Mermaids clapped and did a jig,
As dolphins leaped, oh what a gig!

Refuges in Sapphire Shadows

In the shadows of the coral maze,
Swam a turtle with a splendid gaze.
He wore a cap, quite out of style,
Bobbing along with a lopsided smile.

Starfish lounged, splayed out like a rug,
Reciting poems while giving a shrug.
Bubble parties lit up the scene,
With jellyfish glowing in colors obscene!

The Harmony of Tides and Stars

The tide rolled in with a splishy splash,
As crabs and clams made a great big clash.
'Time for a dance!' a clam did declare,
Dressed in a tutu, he didn't a care.

Stars twinkled down on the water's crest,
As fish threw a party, it was the best.
Mermaids and mermen joined in with cheer,
Singing of laughter, with nothing to fear!

Luminous Lagoon of Serenity

In a lagoon where glowfish gleam,
A crab in a tux has plotted a scheme.
He dances with flair, a top hat on tight,
While seahorses giggle in the moonlight bright.

The jellyfish waltz, with a flick and a flare,
They tango with turtles, a laugh in the air.
A clownfish tells jokes, oh what a delight,
He's the life of the party, all day and night.

Echoes of the Salty Breeze

The seagulls squawk, with sass and with style,
They check their reflections, then add a big smile.
A dolphin comes leaping, a show-off he seems,
Belly flops in the surf, while everyone beams.

The wind sings a tune, with a comical twist,
As fish play charades, not a fin can be missed.
"Look! I'm a penguin!" a goldfish will boast,
While a clam starts to giggle, now that's quite the toast!

Custodians of the Coral Grove

In the coral grove where the colors collide,
A lobster with glasses takes his crabby ride.
He reads all the maps, but never finds land,
Instead, he gets lost in a seaweed band.

A parrotfish paints with a brush made of kelp,
He colors the reef while laughing at help.
"Don't eat my art!" he shouts in distress,
As a grouper approaches, ready for a fest!

Glistening Reflections of Hope

Beneath the waves where the sun's rays do dance,
A starfish attempts a peculiar new prance.
He slips and he slides, what a comical sight,
Watching fish snicker, oh what a delight!

The shrimp hold a party, a bubblegum bash,
With confetti of plankton, they cheer and they dash.
The eels whip their tails, creating a scene,
As everyone giggles in this underwater dream.

Currents of Calm

The boat now sways, oh what a sight,
A seagull steals my sandwich, what a plight.
My sunscreen's thick as glue, I can't see,
I know for sure the fish are laughing at me.

The waves roll by like a clumsy dance,
A crab creeps near, should I take a chance?
He scuttles off with my last fry in tow,
I'll tell my friends it's a tale of woe.

The Lost Kingdom of the Waves

Deep beneath, there's a fish with flair,
Wearing sunglasses, not a single care.
He winks at me, says, "Join the club!"
Offers me seaweed, looks like a grub.

I spot a mermaid with sparkly scales,
She rolls her eyes at the boat's failed sails.
"Stick with me, we'll sip sea foam drinks!"
"Just watch your step, or you'll mess my blinks!"

Glistening Shores of Serenity

Upon the shore, I meet a friendly crab,
He's got a beach ball, but he's such a drab.
He tosses it high, it lands on my head,
I laugh so hard, I forget where I tread.

The sand is warm, but my feet are hot,
I dance around, looking quite the klutzy spot.
The ocean giggles, 'Come take a dip!'
I plop right in and do an awkward flip!

Whispering Shells of Joy

I pick up a shell, it whispers my name,
"Stop looking grumpy, it's all just a game!"
I chuckle out loud, startling a fish,
He blows bubbles at me, what a funny wish!

The tide comes in, and I lose my shoe,
A seagull swoops down, keen for a chew.
"That's my snack!" I holler across the shore,
But he just giggles, as he seeks out more.

Chasing Horizons in Fluid Light

Waves dance under the sun's bright face,
I tripped on a jellyfish, oh what a race!
Seagulls squawk tunes, a cacophony's feat,
Their squawking a tune, who's got the beat?

Flip-flops flying, as I make my escape,
While my hat does a twirl, in terrible shape.
With laughter and splashes, the ocean my friend,
Oh, joy and disaster, together they blend!

Elegy of the Celestial Sea

A fish in a tux, quite dapper and neat,
Asked for a dance, well, that's hard to beat!
With bubbles of laughter, and seaweed in tow,
Can a crab do the cha-cha? I'd love to know.

Tides bring in treasures, like flip-flops and shells,
Mermaids are laughing, oh can't you just tell?
As I sip on my drink, a surprise takes its course,
A shark in a bowtie? Oh, that's quite the source!

Lavish Shores of Myth and Legend

On shores of gold, where legends delight,
I saw a sea turtle taking a flight.
He wore a top hat, so classy, I'd say,
But still, he was late — well, turtles do play.

With krakens and pirates, my friends for the day,
We laughed as they bickered, in their own silly way.
They fought over treasure, which turned out to be
A chest full of toys – oh, what a sight to see!

Crystalline Shores of Tranquility

Under crystalline skies, I napped with a grin,
While waves whispered secrets, oh let the fun begin!
A crab made a hat, from seaweed and foam,
Declared he would host, saying, "Welcome to home!"

As shells danced around, in a curious spree,
An octopus juggled, oh what a sight to see!
With laughter and chuckles, the sun began to sink,
In this quirky seaside, I'm glad I can think!

Where Ocean Meets the Sky

The seagulls squawk as I take a dip,
A splash, a slip, now I've lost my grip.
My sunscreen's gone, and I look like a fry,
But who needs fashion when dolphins swim by?

Shells in my pocket, one left on the sand,
I try to build castles, but they just won't stand.
A crab looks at me, all pincers and sass,
Saying, 'You're too slow; just let the tide pass.'

The sun's blazing down, my drink's flowing free,
I slurp it all up, where's the umbrella for me?
With waves at my feet and sand in my toes,
I laugh at my sunburn—why do I pose?

As sunset approaches, I spot a great whale,
It bounces up high; oh what a tail!
Laughter erupts as we dance with the breeze,
In this wacky place, naught but joy and ease.

Transcendent Tides

Here comes the tide with a giggle and splash,
It tickles my ankles, makes a mad dash.
As I chase the waves, I trip and I roll,
The ocean's my jester, losing all control.

My ice cream's melting, what a sticky mess,
A seagull swoops down, stealing my dress.
He thinks it's a snack, oh what a prior,
Next time I'll wear my old swimwear attire.

The sunset glimmers, a show on the stage,
As I dance with the shadows, my thoughts disengage.
A beach ball flies past, I take a big chance,
I catch it with flair—now let's start a dance!

With each crazy wave, the laughter abounds,
In this ocean of fun, joy forever surrounds.
Clip-clop of my flip-flops, a melody sweet,
I'll wade through the dreams left behind with my feet.

Celestial Shores Await

The sun in the sky gives me a bright wink,
As I chew on sandcastles, what will I think?
My hat's blown away, it's off with a catch,
A seagull too cheeky finds it quite fetching, a match.

Kites flying high, twisting in the breeze,
My sandwich is gone, eaten by the sea bees.
Oh what's that in the waves—an eel with a hat?
He wobbles and flops, 'You call this a chat?'

I'm diving for treasures of glitter and gold,
But it's just an old flip-flop, or so I've been told.
The tide giggles softly, the sky's in a whirl,
Making funny fish faces; ah, he gives it a twirl!

As day turns to night, the stars come to play,
I laugh with the moon at the end of the day.
Ocean's my playground, with friends all around,
In this silly retreat, pure joy can be found.

Echoes of a Distant Isle

On a distant isle where the coconuts grow,
I try to climb high, but my luck's running low.
The palms bend and sway; they giggle at me,
While I tumble and trip down to salty debris.

Can't find my hat; oh what a plight,
The waves toss it back, taking off in flight.
A crab looks at me, a master of guile,
With a sideways salute, he says, 'Stay a while!'

Joining the fishes, I swim like a clown,
In circles and spins, I just float upside down.
A dolphin pops up with a joke so absurd,
"Catch me if you can!" Hilarious bird!

The sun begins fading, the colors so bright,
As laughter and waves dance to the night light.
With fond silly moments on this whimsical spree,
I revel in joy such as this—just me and the sea!

The Lure of Endless Waters

Bobbing like a cork on waves of cheer,
I dream of fish who dance, oh dear!
Seagulls squawk, and they seem to tease,
'Where's your boat? Just float with ease!'

Sunshine drips like honey from the sky,
I lost my snacks; the crabs are sly.
They scuttle near, I beg them, 'No!
Let's share a feast; I've got no dough.'

My flip-flops fly like planes in flight,
Chasing the tide, what a silly sight!
A dolphin grins with a splash and flip,
'Join the fun, take a dip or skip!'

As sunset paints the ocean gold,
I tell my tale, a bit too bold.
Then I trip and fall right off the dock,
And stir the waters with a giggling shock!

Castaway from the Storm

Caught in a tempest, oh what a ride,
My stomach's churning, I tried to hide.
The waves like llamas, wild and free,
Spitting me out like a lost marooned bee!

My ship's a paper boat, it tore apart,
With holes big enough for a curious shark.
I waved at dolphins, they laughed aloud,
'Hey mate, wanna join our fishy crowd?'

Stranded on this sandy mound,
Seagulls stole my lunch; oh, how profound!
I hailed a passing crab for aid,
He winked at me, 'Dude, you've got it made!'

Rain clouds parted, a rainbow appeared,
I danced like a fool, then disappeared.
My beachy throne made of driftwood sticks,
A true castaway, playing silly tricks!

Tranquility amongst the Tides

Sipping coconut from a funky straw,
I chuckle at crabs with no sense of awe.
Tides beckon gently, rolling in and out,
While I twirl my shades, feeling like a lout.

The surf confesses, 'We're all just foam,
Chasing sun rays, never stuck at home.'
And I replied with a chuckle so loud,
'Sean does it best, he's a lazy cloud!'

With flip-flops flapping, I spy a fish,
It winked at me; I made a wish.
To swim with whales and dance with eels,
To find a pirate's treasure that's made of meals!

A toucan fell with a funny squawk,
It landed near me, a talkative rock.
Together we giggle as the sun bows down,
In this silly haven, I wear the crown!

Driftwood Reflections

On a driftwood throne, feeling quite grand,
I contemplate snacks found on the sand.
Ghost crabs scuttling, I join their parade,
As they fight over fries I collywobbled!

The waves are my buddies, we surf and slide,
They tell me secrets about the tide.
I shout back, 'Dude, let's create a splash!'
And the ocean replies with a deluge of cash.

Fins and shells with polka dots stride,
I thought I saw a mermaid, but it's just pride.
Fluffy clouds giggle above my head,
As I roast marshmallows, no reason to dread!

In this silly surf I find my bliss,
Each wave's a hug, every splash a kiss.
And when I faceplant into the brine,
I just laugh aloud; the joy's all mine!

Beneath the Surface of Dreams

A fish in a tux and a crab in a hat,
They dance on the waves, oh how about that!
Seashells wearing sunglasses, so bright and so cool,
Schooling with laughter, it's quite the fine school.

With jellyfish juggling, the show's a delight,
They twirl in the moonlight, a beautiful sight.
Starfish hold hands while the dolphins do flips,
Mermaids serve cocktails and humorous quips.

Whimsical Waters on the Edge

Seagulls sport feathers of colors so wild,
Squawking loud jokes, they delight every child.
Waves do a jig while the sandcastles cheer,
A crab plays the flute, oh, lend me your ear!

The octopus whispers with eight-handed charm,
He tells of a treasure – no one should disarm.
A whale wears a bowtie, he's ready to sing,
While turtles call dibs on the best of the bling.

The Bright Horizon Beckons

The sun wears a crown made of lemons and rays,
Shining a smile through the fog of the bays.
A parrot in slippers, he dances on air,
With a wink and a squawk, he spreads simple flair.

Fish with bright colors, they swim in a line,
They wave to the tourists, all sipping on brine.
The surfboards are laughing, they ride with a grin,
As the tides chuckle softly, let the fun begin!

Embrace of the Tidal Whisper

The whispering waves tease the shores with their tales,
Tickling the toes of the swimming nailails.
A clam tells a story of the great sea parade,
Where turtles walk fashion with the flair they've made.

Anemones bounce in their groovy sea dance,
With snails hitting rhythms, they groove in a trance.
The horizon rolls in with a raucous laugh,
A treasure chest opens, here's an octopus bath!

The Altar of the Waves' Embrace

The waves wear crowns made of froth,
While fish dance like they're on a troth.
Seagulls squawk their funny oaths,
As crabs tap dance on sandy cloths.

In flip-flops, we shuffle about,
While sunburnt tourists scream and shout.
A turtle winks, then steals a snack,
As dolphins giggle, then swim back.

Coconuts fall like bits of fate,
And seaweed hats seem rather great.
Oh buoyant breeze, please don't be shy,
Let's ride the waves, or at least try!

At dusk, we toast to salty jest,
With drinks that jiggle, what a fest!
So here's to waves, in their wild race,
And life's own altar—what a place!

Serendipity at Dusk

As sunset paints the ocean gold,
I chase a school of fish so bold.
They flash and tease in quick retreat,
I trip on shells, oh, what a feat!

A crab with swagger waves its claws,
While boats bob gently, breaking laws.
"Oh no, sir! Don't disturb my nap!"
Cried one who wore a sunhat flap.

The catching sun, a sight so sweet,
With cocktails served in cups of peat.
We toast to stars with paper straws,
While laughter rises, hoots, and paws.

At twilight's hour, we dance on foam,
With every splash, we feel at home.
Oh joy! The beach, our crazy muse,
Where serendipity we choose!

Liquid Dreams Understarred Skies

Beneath the stars, the waves are bright,
Liquid dreams swirl in soft moonlight.
A fishing pole serves as my throne,
As sea creatures laugh at jokes unknown.

Squid sing songs of nautical glee,
While jellyfish float quite effortlessly.
Lobsters wear shades, no need for dives,
As starfish act like they're on five lives.

Sandcastles rise, then tumble down,
As shrimp don tiny hats, what a crown!
"Is that a splash or just a tease?"
The waves reply with bubbly ease.

So here's to nights where fun's the plan,
With laughter that's as vast as the span.
Under the stars, let our dreams fly,
As we dive deep into the sky!

Radiant Isles of Hopeful Mirth

On radiant isles, we sip our cheer,
With crackling laughter ringing near.
A parrot mimics in jesting tone,
As we toast to joys we call our own.

Lobsters strut in a conga line,
While cocktails sparkle like rare wine.
Seashells chorus in casual rhyme,
In sunsets wrapped with whispers of time.

Hammocks sway, as if in trance,
While crabs engage in dance-a-chance.
"Catch me if you can!" they boast and tease,
As they scuttle off with clammy ease.

So raise your glass to fun-filled quests,
In places where the laughter rests.
For here in mirth, we find our way,
In radiant isles, we long to stay!

Celestial Tides Unfurl

The seagulls squawk like jazz bands play,
Dodging waves and sunbeams all day.
Shells tell tales of absent-minded fish,
Who dream of sandcastles, oh what a wish!

Jellyfish twirl in a wobbly dance,
While crabs hold a meeting, given the chance.
The starfish lounge with a smirk on their face,
"Don't bother us, we're enjoying this space!"

A dolphin jokes, "I'm just a shark in disguise,"
As anglers giggle, and fishermen rise.
Spritzing water, all filled with glee,
That slippery tales spun are totally free!

So come on down to the brackish blue,
Where laughter bubbles and dreams sprout anew.
With beach balls in hand and sun hats so bright,
Join the wave party from morning till night!

An Odyssey of Aquatic Dreams

In the calm of the surf, where dreams drift away,
A clam-shaped booth sells 'clams-on-a-balay'.
Mermaids queue for a selfie at dusk,
With octopus stylists, oh what a must!

Seashell phones ring, "Hey, is this the tide?"
"Yeah, it's the ocean, come take a ride!"
Turtles in shades strut along the beach,
While sandcastles wobble, within bubble's reach.

"Watch out for the splash!" warns a crab in a snap,
As a wave rolls in and flips the map.
Fish gossip wildly about the human race,
"Why do they wear such strange things on their face?"

But under the moon's glow, the jesters will sing,
Of pilfered treasure and seaweed bling.
So raise your glass, to laughter's own stream,
For this world of winks is more than a dream!

The Tranquil Horizon's Embrace

A beach ball bounces, it's quite the delight,
But careful, my friend, it just took flight!
The sun wears shades, and the waves hum a tune,
While surfers chat secret plans with the moon.

Walruses sunbathe in hats far too small,
While seahorses giggle, "We're cute, after all!"
The reef's a splendid, wacky parade,
With fish in tuxedos, all slyly displayed.

A clam's sweet serenade lures in the crowd,
As barnacles whisper, "Man, aren't we proud?"
The echoing laughter, a wave in the breeze,
Palms sway along, shaking off all unease.

So, join the jubilee, beneath golden rays,
Where happiness dwells in odd, dreamy ways.
With splashes of laughter rolling over the shore,
It's the sweet taste of ocean, begging for more!

Emerald Depths of Joy

In the emerald hue where the bubbles take flight,
A fish-tastic party kicks off every night!
Grouchy old crabs trade their frowns for a grin,
While clumsy jellybeans boogie and spin.

"Sea cucumber smoothie?" a mermaid will shout,
As dolphins break dance, causing giggles throughout.
Floppy seaweed wigs wave like they're alive,
While snappy little clams join the 'conch' jive.

Octopus jugglers toss shells in delight,
As shrimp in tuxedos chatter through the night.
They'll tell you mad stories of shipwrecks and loot,
With treasures galore, sparkling on the route.

So pull up a starfish, and share in the fun,
This deep-sea cabaret has only begun!
With giggles and splashes, we'll dance and we'll play,
In the oceanic theater, no worries today!

Petals of Foam on the Waves

Sandy toes waltz on the breeze,
Gulls dive-bomb snacks, if you please.
A beach ball bounces, oh what a sight,
Laughter erupts, it's pure delight.

Sunburned faces, a lobster parade,
Sipping cold drinks from a coconut jade.
Mermaids giggle, their tails in a twist,
Waves splash the party, you get the gist.

Seashells piled high like a tower of doom,
Crabs in tuxedos arrive with a zoom.
Tanning is fine, but watch for the tide,
The water a sneaky, slippery slide!

At dusk the fire pits glow with cheer,
Roasting marshmallows, we gather near.
The moonlight chuckles, it knows our glee,
Floating on laughter, just you and me.

The Twinkling Shoreline's Song

Starfish dancing on the soft sand,
Flip-flops flapping, they follow the band.
A seashell choir sings curious tunes,
Under the watch of the sun and the moons.

Beach towels laid out like a patchwork quilt,
A picnic of snacks that the seagulls have spilt.
Soaking it in like a sponge on a spree,
Who knew that beach life was such a glee?

Tides that tumble like a playful child,
Sandcastles crumble, and laughter runs wild.
Grandpa's lost in the waves with a shout,
Surfboards and sunscreen, fun all about!

As night falls, the fire's warm glow,
S'mores in hand, we're putting on a show.
With giggles and tales in the cool evening air,
The night wraps around us, a soft, fluffy chair.

Embers of Sunlight on Liquid Glass

A boat made of laughter sails the blue sea,
Fish wearing sunglasses swim wild and free.
The captain's a parrot, squawking away,
Driving us straight into a bright day.

Ice cream cones drip like a melted dream,
Sunscreen battles, it's a slippery theme.
Dolphins leap over, trying to impress,
We cheer them on, in a sun-kissed mess.

Waves that tickle and splash on my toes,
Seashells whisper secrets, nobody knows.
Beach games invented on a whim and a dare,
Watch out for seagulls, they want your spare!

When twilight dances on shimmering waves,
The ocean whispers tales of brave knaves.
With giggles like bubbles, we toast to the sun,
The day's just begun; oh, what fun to run!

Reflections of an Aquatic Eden

The horizon sprinkles glitter on the blue,
Fish wearing party hats swim in our view.
A beach chair brigade sets up for the laughs,
With sunscreen warriors and silly photographs.

Seagulls swoop in for a crumb-filled feast,
Chasing each other like it's a big beast.
Sandcastles rising like skyscraper dreams,
While kids arm-wrestle with spaghetti ice creams.

Flip-flops abandoned, buried in the sand,
Where crabby friends stick together, hand in hand.
The sun showers warmth, like a tickling breeze,
Leaving us giggling, doing just as we please.

As stars peek out, and the moon takes charge,
We roast marshmallows, making the night large.
With joy and mischief in the salty air,
Life feels like laughter, more than a dare.

Utopian Shores in the Morning Light

Seagulls squawk and steal my fries,
The ocean's dance, a grand surprise.
Sun-kissed waves in laughter roll,
A crab attempts to take a stroll.

Bikini tops and flip-flops fly,
As kids construct a castle high.
A wave crashes down, it vanquishes,
Our kingdom made of soggy wishes.

Tanned sunbathers with sunscreen smears,
Contemplate life through salty sneers.
Barbecue smoke and laughter blend,
A day at sea, where fun won't end!

In boats that wobble like jelly beans,
We fish for laughs, not for cuisine.
With mermaids giggling just out of sight,
We found the joy in morning light.

Whispered Secrets of the Sea

Flippers flop, a dolphin stares,
He's plotting food, maybe some pears.
The waves whisper tales of lost gold,
And stories of sailors, so brave, so bold.

Seashells laugh with each little crunch,
As my friends munch sandwiches for lunch.
The tide pulls me in, it loves to tease,
Like a surly cat who won't say please.

Underwater, fish form a conga line,
While I stumble, awkward but fine.
They twirl around, as jellyfish wave,
My flailing dance, a sight to save!

With a chilly splash, I'm drenched head to toe,
That sea has secrets I'll never know.
But laughter rings, oh what a thrill,
In waves of joy, let's sip and chill.

Rhythms of the Oceanic Tide

The ocean's heartbeat, thump-thump and sway,
It calls to beachgoers here to play.
Crash of surf is a song so grand,
I lose my hat, it flies off to land!

Tsunami of giggles, a seagull troupe,
Dives for snacks with such bold swoop.
The tide rolls in with a comical kiss,
Socks and sandals, a watery bliss!

Surfboards wobble, we stand, we fall,
While seaweed drapes like a weird shawl.
With each wipeout, cheers fill the air,
Who knew the ocean had such flair?

And when the sun dips low and wide,
We embrace the waves like a joyful ride.
With sand in our toes, the fun won't subside,
In the rhythms here, we all take pride.

Halos of Blue Surround the Stillness

Under skies of azure, my mind takes flight,
The sea's infinite blue feels just right.
A floating donut? Is that a seal?
Or just my friend trying to conceal!

Sunbeams dance on water with glee,
While I test out my best cannonball spree.
The splash might drown fish, it's quite a sight,
But laughter erupts—oh what delight!

Beachside loungers wear shades with pride,
As they sip sweet drinks and let time glide.
Seasocks fly as the wind takes a turn,
While everyone giggles at my sunburn!

Clouds turn to cotton candy above,
In this world, all's easy—just like a dove.
With halos of blue, let the fun be crowned,
In this quirky space, true joy is found.

The Heartbeat of the Deep Blue

In waters wide, a fish wore specs,
He gave a wink, what a strange hex.
A crab danced wildly on the sand,
Thinking it was a live rock band.

Starfish held auditions, quite a scene,
For a troupe called 'The Ocean's Dream.'
They twirled through bubbles, bright and bold,
With stories of treasures, long lost gold.

The jellyfish boogied, what a sight,
While seahorses raced, full of delight.
A clam yelled, "Hey, stop that quick spin!"
"I'm trying to nap, where do I begin?"

As waves giggled, the sun shone low,
The sea life partied, putting on a show.
With laughter echoing from reef to shore,
In the deep blue heart, joy forevermore.

Odyssey of the Enchanted Pearl

A pearl once dreamed it was a queen,
Stuck in a shell, feeling quite keen.
With fish as subjects, a crown of kelp,
She ruled the tide with a whimsical yelp.

The octopus wore a top hat for flair,
With dapper moves, he caused quite a scare.
"Oh dear," said the oyster, in a shock,
"Why can't you keep it down, you silly rock?"

The sea turtles tossed confetti and glee,
A birthday bash for the pearl, yippee!
With laughing dolphins diving so high,
Even the gulls called it a 'Wee-Hoo!' fly.

"Dance with me, oh spongy delight,"
Cried the sea cucumber, twirling the night.
With bubbles of joy and glittering light,
An underwater ball, what a whimsical sight!

Humming of Coastal Bliss

With beach balls bouncing, laughter soared,
A crab just couldn't find its hoard.
"Who's stolen my snacks?" it cried in dismay,
The gulls just chuckled, "You'll find them today!"

The tides brought in a stray rubber duck,
Paddling proudly, thinking it's luck.
"Float with me," said a seagull with glee,
"Let's start a trend, just you wait and see!"

Then came a whale with a boombox on fin,
Cranking the tunes, it made the sea spin.
"Throw your fins up! Let's dance till we drop,"
The whole ocean moved, ready to bop!

In coastal bliss, they laughed and they played,
As jellybeans swirled in the sunshine's parade.
With creatures of whimsy in every space,
A beachfront rave, oh what a place!

Sparkling Sanctuaries of Wonder

In coral castles, the fish got dressed,
For a sparkling gala, they felt quite blessed.
A flamboyant flounder showed off his flair,
While a parrotfish laughed, tossing color in the air.

Anemones bounced, full of zest,
Inviting all creatures; it was quite the fest.
With shells as chairs, and seaweed for ties,
They feasted on plankton under starry skies.

"Oh dear!" cried a clam with a twitch of its shell,
"Who stepped on my toes? Can't you tell?"
As snails slid by in their casual glide,
Making waves in the party, laughter worldwide.

Bubbles popped like confetti in flight,
With giggles erupting from morning to night.
In this sanctuary where fun never drifted,
The ocean's heart danced, and spirits were lifted.

A Symphony of Salty Breezes

Seagulls squawk, a concert loud,
With flip-flops playing in the crowd.
A crab conducts with a sideways dance,
While waves clap hands in a foamy trance.

The sun's a DJ, spinning bright,
As sunbathers groove from left to right.
Shells join in, a rhythmic blend,
With laughter echoing, fun won't end.

Picnics spread, snacks take flight,
Sandcastles topple in sheer delight.
A beach ball bounces, what a brawl,
As kids go diving, heed the call!

Life's a treasure, salt in the air,
With sunscreen splatters everywhere.
In this whimsical, wild retreat,
Every moment is a tasty treat.

Secrets Behind the Surf

Fish whisper secrets, tales of old,
Of mermaids singing, bold and gold.
A dolphin giggles, flips in glee,
As waves tickle toes, come join and see!

Sandcastles built with royal flair,
Guarded by crabs who don't have a care.
The tide sneaks up, gives them a wash,
As sand engineers come back and frolic.

Surfboards queue for their daring ride,
Wipeouts end with a splashing slide.
A clam with shades takes in the show,
While jellyfish float with a graceful flow.

The horizon beckons with a wink,
As laughter floats on the ocean's brink.
In sunny mischief, tales are spun,
With secrets hidden, but oh what fun!

Stars Dancing on the Water

At dusk, the water starts to glow,
As starfish twinkle, putting on a show.
With moonbeams jiving on the swell,
The ocean hums a playful spell.

Crabs in tuxedos waltz with pride,
While fish in sequins take a glide.
A splash of laughter, a twirl in the waves,
As sea cucumbers sway like brave knaves.

The horizon blushes, sunset's kiss,
While goofy sea turtles can't help but miss.
The night sky's the limit, laughter's the star,
In this dance of joy, no one's too far.

As surfboards glide, and laughter rings,
A comet dives, oh, the joy it brings!
With each wave crashing, life's a dance,
Embrace the fun, come take a chance!

Floating on Gentle Wishes

A hammock swings, the clouds float by,
A seagull's joke makes the sun blurt a sigh.
Coconut drinks with tiny umbrellas,
Belly laughs burst from group of fellas.

Waves roll in with a scoff and a cheer,
As beach hats fly off, oh dear, oh dear!
Picnic ants march like they own the place,
While I try to catch a wave with grace.

Kites soar high, like dreams on a string,
The ocean's a canvas, let laughter ring.
As jellybeans bounce in the sand,
Life's a treasure, in this sweet land.

The sun dips low, but spirits soar,
With dance and wit, we all want more.
Floating wishes, giggles in the air,
In this joyous place, we shed all care.

The Dreamers' Refuge

In a boat made of jelly and dreams,
Gulls squawk like they're plotting schemes.
A fish wears a hat, quite absurd,
And waves giggle, not shy to be heard.

Seagulls mime all the latest trends,
While crabs breakdance; oh, how it bends!
The ocean's laughter, a silly show,
Tickles the toes of the sun below.

Turtles snooze in sun-baked bliss,
While octopuses barter a seaweed kiss.
A dolphin juggles shells with flair,
Sipping seawater from the air.

Mermaids trade fish for a cup of tea,
With a side of seaweed cake, oh me!
In this nook, life's never a bore,
For every wave opens a new door.

Lullaby of the Lapping Waves

Waves rock the boat with a gentle sway,
As barnacles hold their own cabaret.
Crabs sing ballads with pinch and clap,
While starfish lounge, enjoying the nap.

The moon winks down with a glittery grin,
While seaweed sways, stretching in spin.
Clams recite poetry, shells all around,
As the ocean whispers, soft and profound.

Sandcastles crumble with a giggle and splash,
Seashells play poker for a nightly bash.
The tide tells tales of treasures so bold,
As sea otters hoard glittering gold.

With jellyfish twirling in balletic dance,
They paint the water with romance.
In this nighttime show under starry sight,
The ocean hums soft songs of delight.

Colorful Life Beneath the Surface

Beneath the waves, it's quite the scene,
With fish that dazzle and mermaids keen.
A clownfish laughs at a funny joke,
While a pufferfish dreams of becoming bespoke.

Kelp forests waved in a playful jest,
Where seahorses play hide and seek best.
A crab flips pancakes with a flip and a crack,
In this wacky world, who needs a snack?

Anemones dance in a psychedelic swirl,
While octopus chefs create a seafood swirl.
Shrimps serve cocktails in tiny shells,
And dolphins gossip; oh, do they tell!

With jellyfish floating like balloons in the breeze,
The sea turtles fashion themselves as tease.
In this underwater circus of cheer,
Every critter's smile sings loud and clear.

The Horizon's Caress

The sun sets down with a cheeky grin,
As waves pop in with a splashy win.
Sailing boats sport colorful flags,
While fish throw parties in old sea rags.

The horizon blushes with strokes of gold,
As crabs retell tales, all the bold.
Seagulls applaud with a raucous cheer,
For the sunset's art day, so full of cheer.

A dolphin tricks sailors, a playful tease,
While mermaids sip drinks made from the seas.
With a flip and a swoosh, they dazzle and glide,
In waves of laughter, their spirits abide.

Even the clouds join this merry parade,
As evening unfolds, the stars invade.
With a wink of a lighthouse, a beacon it sends,
Here on the waters, the fun never ends.

Elysium in the Waves

Seagulls squawk in silly tunes,
Shells dance around like little loons.
The fish wear hats and swim so neat,
Crabs play poker, it's quite a feat.

Flip-flops flop on a deck so bare,
Sunburned noses, we've not a care.
Laughter spills like soda pop,
Sandy sandwiches, it's time to stop.

Ocean waves crash with a splashy cheer,
Beach balls sail, oh dear, oh dear!
Mermaids giggle, they lost their fins,
As dolphins tease them with playful grins.

Surfers tumble, riding in style,
Wipeouts bring laughter, oh what a while!
But beware of the rubber duck's attack,
It's the fiercest beast on this beachy track!

The Siren's Embrace

With a wink and a splash, she calls us near,
But her voice is a song that we can't quite hear.
Fish pizza parties make everyone beg,
While jellyfish juggle, what a silly leg!

Her hair flows like noodles in bubbly foam,
We try to swim, but we just float home.
Turtles wear shades, they're cooler than most,
While octopuses twirl and dance like a host.

"Come dance with me!" the siren does cheer,
But she steps on a clam—oh dear, oh dear!
The crabs all applaud, with their pincers they clap,
We're all in stitches, it's quite a mishap!

When the sun sets low, she bids us goodbye,
Leaving behind just a wink and a sigh.
Mermaid mayhem and laughter abide,
In waters so silly, you can't help but glide!

Nautical Dreams Unfurled

Sailing along in a boat made of cheese,
The captain's a cat with plans to tease.
A map drawn by crabs leads to a snack,
With jellybeans hidden in the hull's back.

Stars sprinkle confetti in the night sky,
Where dolphins wear tuxes and dance not shy.
Fish take the helm, wearing sailor hats,
While seagulls squawk jokes with clever chats.

The anchor is missing, floated away,
All hands on deck, but they'll just play.
Cannonballs burst into sugary treats,
And pirates end up on treetop seats!

With dreams of lollipops and candy canes,
We sail along, avoiding the rains.
A treasure of laughter, so sweet and grand,
In the land of the sea, where fun takes a stand!

Horizon's Whisper

Whispers of waves say, "Come take a ride!"
With surfboards shaped like bananas, we glide.
The tide takes our troubles, swirls them away,
As crabs do a conga, come join the ballet!

Clouds made of marshmallows float in blue grace,
Where fish play hide-and-seek in a race.
Each wave brings a giggle, a bubble, a joke,
While a porpoise plays bass, making us poke.

The horizon glimmers, filled with fun light,
As kites made of cupcakes soar to new heights.
A whale with a bowtie sings us a tune,
While seagulls breakdance, under the moon!

So let's sail away on this whimsical spree,
With laughter and cheer from the ocean's decree.
In salty adventures, our spirits ignite,
As we ride the waves into joyful delight!

A Haven Beneath Clouded Skies

In a boat made of bananas, we sail,
With a crew of raccoons, we'll never fail.
The sun's shy behind clouds, playing hide and seek,
While jellyfish dance, making us feel unique.

Seagulls squawk jokes, they think they're comedians,
Splashing in waves, we're all mermaidedians.
Our anchor's a rubber duck, squishy and bright,
Laughing together, we sail through the night.

The map's upside down, we don't need the stars,
We'll find joy in teacups or run from the jars.
With ice cream for maps, no agenda at hand,
Just sailing on smiles, in this whimsical land.

So grab your flip-flops, let's take to the blue,
Live life as a jest, as a seagull would do.
With snacks from the cooler, we'll feast without care,
Lost in a chuckle, we'll float through the air.

Voyage to the Unseen Promise

Off we go in a ship made of cheese,
With a captain who sneezes and dances with ease.
The wind plays the tunes, we're all part of the show,
While dolphins throw parties, just go with the flow.

The treasure we seek? A gigantic fish fry,
With shrimp doing summersaults, oh my, oh my!
Sailing on our dreams, under candy floss skies,
Where laughter is currency and joy never dies.

A lighthouse made of cupcakes, it lights up the sea,
Guiding us home where it's always carefree.
We count fluffy clouds, sharing giggles and grins,
In this voyage of whims where the fun never thins.

We'll swap stories with otters, paint rainbows on waves,
Collecting the moments that laughter engraves.
Set sail on a whim, let the shenanigans run,
This voyage is best when it's all just for fun.

Elysium Beneath the Waves

Beneath waves of giggles, where fish wear bow ties,
Mermaids sell cupcakes and swim with surprise.
Octopuses juggling, what a sight to behold,
In this underwater circus, the laughs are gold.

We ride on the backs of the swift dolphins bright,
Skipping through coral, it's a pure delight.
Sea turtles are painting with brushes made of kelp,
This oceanic laughter is a wave of pure help.

The jellybean jellyfish float by like they know,
While crabs dance the cha-cha, putting on a show.
We splash in the bubbles, chasing our dreams,
Where laughter's a treasure, bursting at the seams.

Let's toast to the sea, in our fizzy seashell cups,
With cheers from the starfish, and playful hiccup ups.
In this watery realm, where silliness thrives,
We find our true joy, where the laughter dives.

Shores of Serendipity

On shores made of marshmallows, we kick off our shoes,
With sand made of sprinkles, we've nothing to lose.
The sun in a sombrero gives us a warm wink,
While crabs polish shells and playfully blink.

The tide tickles toes with a giggly embrace,
And the seaweed wiggles in joyful grace.
With seashells for trumpets, we beat out a tune,
Under a wobbly sky, a bright and silly moon.

Surfboards made of pizza drift into play,
As fish wear sunglasses in the sun's warm ray.
We build castles of candy, a sweet little spree,
On shores of pure laughter, so wild and so free.

So let's dance with the waves and sing to the breeze,
On this comical shore, life is always a tease.
With every bobbing wave, happiness flows,
In this land of odd wonders, where silliness grows.

The Search for Eden's Edge

In a boat with a funny crew,
We sailed the waves of bright blue.
Tales of treasure guided us there,
With jokes that filled the salty air.

Seagulls squawking, diving for fries,
While fish wear sunglasses, oh what a surprise!
We danced with dolphins, jumped like fools,
In waters that sparkled, breaking all rules.

We searched for coconuts dressed in crowns,
And found a crab who told us of towns.
His gossip was salty, his wit not bland,
In our boat full of laughter, we sailed hand in hand.

With every wave, we splashed and played,
Creating a ruckus that would never fade.
The quest for the edge became one great jest,
In humor and joy, we found our best.

Tranquil Waters of Enchanted Landscapes

In tranquil glades where the water glows,
We paddled a canoe, where nobody knows.
A fish with a hat swam by with delight,
Singing silly songs in the morning light.

The reeds were swaying in a gentle cheer,
As frogs in tuxedos croaked jokes to hear.
Our snacks went flying as the wind took flight,
While turtles played poker, oh what a sight!

Chasing the waves, we splashed around,
With laughter echoing, what fun we found!
The maps were all wrong, yet we didn't mind,
For adventure and chuckles were perfectly signed.

At dusk we camped, our fire aglow,
With tales of mermaids and the winds of woe.
In those tranquil waters, our hearts felt bright,
As we played with the magic of the endless night.

A Voyage to the Unseen Isles

Setting sail for isles of great bliss,
We packed some snacks, how could we miss?
With a parrot who spoke in riddles and rhymes,
We laughed our way through the most silly times.

Each isle we found had its own quirky tea,
With flavors like laughter and giggles, you see.
A crab made us hats from seaweed and shells,
While mermaids rehearsed their stand-up, oh swell!

We searched for treasures of chocolate gold,
But found jellybeans, a sight to behold!
This adventure was crazy, but oh what a thrill,
Sailing onwards with laughter, we couldn't be still.

We danced with the waves, made friends with the tide,
In our boat full of joy, we took it in stride.
For in the unseen, we found silly fun,
And knew this wild voyage had only begun.

Mystical Journey through Oceanic Dreams

On a mystical journey through dreams and schemes,
We sailed with a crew of unicorn beams.
The ocean was winking, a real cheeky tease,
As we laughed with the jellyfish swaying at ease.

Each wave whispered secrets, each splash brought a grin,
As we chatted with octopuses trying to win.
They challenged us games of chess on the reef,
While sea cows told tales that brought us great grief.

The wind played guitar, a magical sound,
As boats turned to disco and danced all around.
With stars in our eyes and dreams on our tongue,
We sang silly ballads, forever young.

In this ocean of dreams, hilarity soared,
Each moment a treasure, each giggle adored.
Our mystical journey, with joy bubbling high,
Left us with memories that danced in the sky.

Cherished Moments adrift

We sailed on a boat made of dreams,
With snacks that were bursting at the seams.
The seagulls squawked, stealing our fries,
While we laughed at their sneaky surprise.

Tons of jellyfish danced in a row,
Calling us over to join in the show.
We jumped in the waves, like fish out of air,
While a crab made a face, like he didn't care.

A dolphin popped up, wearing a hat,
Said, "You're quite odd, but where's the cat?"
We offered our kite, it flew like a breeze,
And the wind just laughed, as if to tease.

Now memories swirl like salt in the sea,
Inky squid sketches after our spree.
With each wave that crashes, we smile and shout,
"Who needs a map? We're lost, but it's out!"

The Sea's Secret Haven

Beneath the sun, we found our nook,
A hidden cove, like a storybook.
Starfish giggled as we walked by,
Tickling our toes, saying, "Oh my!"

The waves whispered tales from faraway lands,
Only to be interrupted by jellyfish bands.
We danced with the turtles, oh what a sight,
Twisting and turning with all our might.

A crab stole our sandwich, what a fine thief,
Finding joy in our chips like a comic relief.
We warned him to stop, but he gave us a wink,
And scuttled away, quicker than we could blink.

With treasure maps drawn in the sand,
Plotting adventures, oh, weren't we grand!
Every wave crested with laughter and cheer,
In our secret haven, there's nothing to fear.

Beneath the Infinite Blue

Under hues of blue, our boat set sail,
Chasing the sunset, we followed the trail.
A fish in a bowtie approached with a grin,
"Care to join me for some fun in the fin?"

We splashed and flipped like acrobats wild,
Laughing at mischief, just like a child.
The whales sang songs, but out of tune,
Still, we cheered them on, high-fiving the moon.

A parrot in colors that stunned the eye,
Said, "You folks are cracked! Come give it a try."
With each comical twist, a new dare was made,
And we felt the salt air, our worries outweighed.

In waters that giggled, we let our hearts roam,
Crafting wild stories, far away from home.
Beneath that blue, we floated and played,
In a world of giggles, our worries betrayed.

A Journey to Solace

On a wooden raft, we drifted along,
Matching our silliness to sea's silly song.
The turtles looked puzzled, as we passed them by,
"Are you lost or just looking?!" they seemed to cry.

We fished for laughter with nets made of fun,
Catch of the day? Just sunburn and puns!
The crabs threw a party and danced with glee,
A conga line formed – join in—you'll see!

With every soft wave, our worries did flee,
As sea foam tickled toes, saying, "You're free!"
A mermaid laughed loud, "Nice haircut, my friend!"
And we twirled like whirligigs, hearts on the mend.

In this quirky journey, we found our way,
Amidst giggles and splashes, come what may.
For solace was never a faraway claim,
It was here in the sea, where we played the game.

Ephemeral Islands of Delight

In a boat made of candy and dreams,
We sail past the islands with strawberry streams.
The seagulls wear hats, and they squawk with glee,
As they steal our snacks, those rascals at sea.

Every wave tells a joke with a splash,
A fish winks at us, oh how it's brash!
With jellyfish dancing in tutus so bright,
We laugh till we cry, what a wonderful sight!

A treasure map scribbled in whip cream and sand,
Leads us to cocktails from a pirate's own hand.
The sandcastle kings declare us their mates,
As we feast on their bounty—no need for debates.

When the sun sets below the horizon so wide,
The mermaids invite us for a wild midnight ride.
With laughter and music, we float on the tide,
In this realm of fine folly, joy can't be denied!

Enchanted Waters of the Soul

On a splashy old raft, what a ride it can be,
With dolphins doing flips, it's laugh therapy!
The crab in a bowtie serves drinks with a grin,
While octopuses juggle, their talent's a win.

We tiptoe on waves made of cotton candy,
Sailing through fluff where it's always dandy.
A parade of odd fish with sequined scales,
Sings goofy songs of their comical tales.

The sunbeam bandana tied snug on my head,
As I sit back and chuckle, no worries or dread.
With each tickling wave, I snort and I squawk,
The sea's full of laughter, a non-stop talk!

As night blankets water in shimmering light,
The stars join the party, what a glorious sight!
In this magical realm, we chuckle and play,
Forever in joy—let the laughter sway!

The Dance of Seraphic Waves

Waves do a jig, all caught in a spin,
Seashells are clapping, let the dance begin!
Jellybeans bobbing, a colorful swarm,
As we join in the fun, it's a bubbly warm.

Crabs with their maracas, a rhythmic delight,
Tap-dancing sea stars twinkling so bright.
Gulls wear tutus, oh what a grand show,
The ocean's a stage, and we're part of the flow.

With taffy-stuffed treasure, we twirl and we whirl,
Laughing at fish who just want to unfurl.
Mermaids with smiles harmonize under the moon,
The night turns to magic, we're over the moon!

Oh, the sea is a joke in a mischievous mask,
With each wave that laughs, we forget every task.
In this frolicking dream, we twine and we leap,
For the dance of the waves never lets us sleep!

Radiance of the Infinite Blue

In a realm of bright azure, we sail with a cheer,
With sun hats and sunblock, adventure is near.
The fish in tuxedos hold fancy galas,
And we're all invited—what fun for the balas!

The seabreeze blows kisses, with a wink and a tease,
While the jellyfish giggle with touches of breeze.
We ride on the plankton, a wild, silly dance,
As waves hurl us forward, it's the best merry prance!

With ice cream cones melting, we shriek and we laugh,
Seagulls steal fries, and we're left with half.
But who needs a meal when the joy is so stout,
In this carnival sea, of silliness, we shout!

Beneath the bright skies, oh what a delight,
With whims of the ocean, we'll party all night.
Cheers to the splashes that tickle our feet,
For the happiness found here is pretty hard to beat!

Celestial Currents

In a boat made of jelly, we drift on a whim,
The gulls feast on popcorn, our chances look slim.
A crab plays the banjo, it's quite a tough crowd,
As we laugh at the seagulls who squawk way too loud.

The fish start a conga, they dance to the tide,
A dolphin escapes, our tour guide, he cried.
With sunscreen as armor, we lounge like true pros,
While jellyfish giggle at our silly pose.

A treasure map found, leads straight to a pie,
But the pirate's got crumbs, and the pie's turning dry.
We trade jokes with the mermaids, who sip on sweet tea,
As the waves carry laughter, wild and carefree.

In a world made of giggles, we float like a dream,
While octopus chefs whip up a wacky ice cream.
In celestial waters, we splash 'til it's dark,
And our hearts sail away, lit by whimsy's spark.

Sunlit Sanctuaries

On umbrellas of pizza, we sunbathe with glee,
With sunbeams as toppings, we live quite carefree.
A parrot named Louie, he talks just like me,
And he bakes in the sun, quite joyfully free.

We built a grand castle, of sand and of laughs,
Where the tide steals our roof, and our frothy cold drafts.
We dive for the sea fries, and catch jellybean dreams,
As fish throw us parties, or so it seems.

With seashells as tickets, we ride on the waves,
Where our thoughts turn to laughter, no time left to save.
The sun dips like ice cream, it's melting away,
As we toast to our fortune, on this hot sunny day.

In sunlit dimensions, we dance with the tide,
With beach goats as buddies, we launch our slide.
We'll store all our chuckles, like crabs with their shells,
In this world full of giggles, where everything swells.

The Alchemy of Aquamarine

A wizard in fins brews a magical brew,
With seaweed as wands, and a fish as his crew.
They conjure up bubbles, of laughter and light,
As the waves crash around, the moment feels right.

With seashells as chalices, we sip salty air,
While seagulls recite poetry, if they dare.
Each splash tells a secret, a riddle, a rhyme,
In waters where giggles are kept in their prime.

We barter with sea turtles, for jokes and for snacks,
While starfish do twirls, with coordinated hacks.
The ocean's a playground, with joy as the key,
Wrapped in waves' laughter, we feel truly free.

At dusk, our adventures sparkle like stars,
As the moon joins our dance, no need for memoirs.
In this alchemy, wonders and chuckles align,
In aquamarine chaos, our hearts intertwine.

Blissful Shores of Reverie

On shores made of giggles, we romp through the sand,
Building towers of candy, so sweet and so grand.
With jumpy sea horses, we leap and we bound,
As the waves splash with laughter, joy all around.

A beach ball named Binky rolls by with a grin,
As we race down the shoreline, let the games begin!
With ice cream for armor and sunhats so bright,
We twirl through the dunes, all day and all night.

The tide tells us tales of lost shoes and fun,
As barnacles cheer for the race we've just run.
With giggles and splashes, the ocean's our mate,
In blissful horizons, we celebrate fate.

As the sun bids goodbye with a wink and a grin,
We gather our treasures, the odd and the chin.
In this land full of laughter, we find joy anew,
On shores of reverie, where wishes come true.

The Symphony of Rolling Waves

The waves rise up like a dancing crew,
Splashing the boat with a frothy brew.
Seagulls squawk like it's karaoke night,
As fish below play hide and seek out of sight.

With salty snacks and sunburned glee,
We wave to the dolphins, they wave back with glee.
The ocean's a stage, the sun's the spotlight,
While jellyfish waltz in the dark of night.

Tangled in nets, a prankster's delight,
A mermaid swims past, giggling at fright.
Her scales shimmer bright, but her hair's a mess,
She blames it on tides; it's her hair's distress.

So dance, oh heart, to the rhythm of splash,
For every mishap, there's always a laugh,
As we float in our boat on this watery stage,
The symphony plays, and we join the age.

Secrets of the Sapphire Deep

In the deep blue where secrets reside,
Octopi play cards, their skill they won't hide.
They ink out deals while fish jump in jest,
Negotiating snacks is their very best quest.

A treasure chest sits, filled with the odd,
Rings made of shells, a sandy old clod.
The crabs tell the tale of a swashbuckler bold,
Who mistook a beach ball for a chest full of gold.

The coral, a city where fish prance about,
Waving hello with a graceful shout.
They gossip of humans who build up the reef,
With plastic and trash, oh, what a belief!

So dive down deep, if you dare take the leap,
Join the whimsical dance, let the ocean keep.
For in layers below, where laughter runs free,
The tales bloom like seaweed, just wait and see!

Everlasting Elegance of the Vista

The horizon stretches, a painter's wild dream,
Where seagulls sport hats and sailboats team.
With every sunset, a giggle erupts,
As splashy waves dance while the sun interrupts.

Tanned tourists laugh 'neath the palm trees' sway,
Competing with coconuts, in a silly fray.
Each sunset's a cue for the beach to have fun,
Cocktails in hand, until the day's done.

The breeze carries whispers of sails on the run,
Of pirate tales wrapped in laughter and sun.
A crab steals a chip from the party quite sly,
While folks waddle after, howling, "Oh my!"

So raise your glass high under skies full of cheer,
For elegance comes with a side of good beer.
The vista unfolds, yet with humor you see,
The laughter's the best part, it's all we agree.

Joyous Isles of Exploration

Off to the islands, where laughter blends sweet,
We sail 'round the coast, with snacks we can eat.
On treasure hunts led by mysterious maps,
We dig for some goodies, or maybe just naps.

Each isle a wonder, with critters galore,
Lizards wear sunglasses, oh, what a score!
While parrots trade stories of ships gone astray,
As we munch on our lunch in the warm light of day.

We climb rocky cliffs, with giggles we leap,
Chasing our shadows, the ocean runs deep.
With sand between toes, and kite strings in hand,
We dance with the waves; together we stand.

For on these bright shores, where joy makes its mark,
Every sunset's a canvas, igniting a spark.
Adventure awaits in this whimsical spree,
As we wade through the laughter, wild and free.

www.ingramcontent.com/pod-product-compliance
Lightning Source LLC
Chambersburg PA
CBHW072223070526
44585CB00015B/1458